curious about
POKÉMON

BY RACHEL GRACK

AMICUS

What are you

curious about?

CHAPTER THREE

Bet You Didn't Know ...

PAGE

16

Curious About is published by Amicus
P.O. Box 227
Mankato, MN 56002
www.amicuspublishing.us

Editor: Alissa Thielges
Series and Book Designer: Kathleen Petelinsek
Cover Designer: Lori Bye
Photo Researcher: Omay Ayres

Library of Congress Cataloging-in-Publication Data
Names: Koestler-Grack, Rachel A., 1973– author.
Title: Curious about Pokémon / by Rachel Grack.
Description: Mankato, MN. Amicus, [2024] | Series: Curious
about favorite brands | Includes bibliographical references
and index. | Audience: Ages 5–9 | Audience: Grades 2–3
| Summary: "Nine kid-friendly questions give elementary
readers an inside look at Pokémon to spark their curiosity
about the brand's history, games, and cultural impact. A
Stay Curious! feature models research skills while simple
infographics support visual literacy."—Provided by publisher.
Identifiers: LCCN 2022032143 (print) | LCCN 2022032144
(ebook) | ISBN 9781645493303 (library binding) | ISBN
9781681528540 (paperback) | ISBN 9781645494188 (ebook)
Subjects: LCSH: Pokémon (Game)—Juvenile
literature. | Video games—Juvenile literature.
Classification: LCC GV1469.35.P63 K64 2024 (print) | LCC
GV1469.35.P63 (ebook) | DDC 794.8—dc23/eng/20220708
LC record available at https://lccn.loc.gov/2022032143
LC ebook record available at https://lccn.loc.gov/2022032144

Photos © Alamy/Album 17, cartoonpub 20; Dreamstime/
Aksitaykut 11 (Onyx, Charizard), 14 (insets), 22, 23, Aykut2607
4 (characters), Lim Seng Kui 6, Mariayunira 11 (Pikachu), Matthew
Corley 10 (hand and phone); Shutterstock/Bruno Ismael Silva
Alves 8, 12–13, Colin Temple 5, COO7 18–19, enchanted_fairy
16, Hannari_eli 11, 14 (bkgd), 15, Hethers 18 (card), I and J
Photography 6–7, Nicescene cover, 1, Mirko Kuzmanovic 21,
QinJin 10 (bkgd), RG-vc 4 (cartridges), Simbert Brause 9

Printed in China

Who invented Pokémon?

Game Freak. It is a video game company. Satoshi Tajiri owns it. As a boy, he searched the forests in Japan for bugs and tadpoles. His adventures became Pokémon games. Instead of bugs, players catch creatures. They train them to battle each other. In 1996, Pokémon made its first video game.

Kids first played Pokémon on the Nintendo Game Boy.

DID YOU KNOW?
Pokémon is short for
POcKEt MONsters.

Players today can
catch and train
Pokémon on a
smart phone.

Was the video game based on the cards?

Nope. The cards came out after the video game. They became very popular. People collected and traded them. Cartoons, movies, and new video games followed. Today, Pokémon is one of the top game **brands** in the world! More than 30 billion Pokémon cards have been printed.

DID YOU KNOW?
Some old Pokémon cards are worth big bucks. In 2022, a rare Pikachu card from 1998 sold for $900,000!

How do I play?

TRAINER NOTES

Trainers choose their six best fighters to do battle.

You can play with the cards or the video games. The goal is the same. You are on a **quest** to become the best Pokémon trainer. Sometimes you travel to **gyms** and face off with other trainers. Your **rival** picks a Pokémon from their deck. You need to beat it. Who should you choose? To win, you must know the Pokémon in your collection.

Name

Evolution Stage

Level

Hit Points

Pokémon Type

Luxray LV.53   HP **120**

STAGE 2 *Evolves from Luxio*

NO. 405 Gleam Eyes Pokémon HT: 4'07" WT: 92.6 lbs.

Pokémon Data

Move Name

Flash   **30**

If the Defending Pokémon tries to attack during your opponent's next turn, your opponent flips a coin. If tails, that attack does nothing.

Gadget Bolt   **60**

If Luxray has a Pokémon Tool card attached to it, you may do 100 damage instead of 60 to the Defending Pokémon. If you do, discard that Pokémon Tool card.

Attack Damage

Attack Description

It can see clearly through walls to track down its prey and seek its lost young.

Character Background

Illus. kawayoo

Illustrator

weakness   resistance   retreat cost

+30   -20

©2009 Pokémon/Nintendo   5/99 ★

Series

Weakness   Resistance   Card Number   Rarity Symbol

Why do players battle their Pokémon?

Mostly for fun! Trainers battle in friendly **competitions**. You can also earn a badge if you beat the gym leader. Collect all the badges, and you are a Pokémon Champion!

Players also fight wild Pokémon to capture them. In Pokémon Go, players catch Pokémon that appear in the real world.

You have to go outside and walk around to play Pokémon Go.

PIKACHU

CHARIZARD

ONYX

MEWTWO

EEVEE

Energy cards make a Pokémon stronger, but the type must match.

Pokémon Type

What is a Pokémon type?

DID YOU KNOW?
There are 18 types.
A Pokémon master
knows them all!

100

It is a group of Pokémon with similar features. For example, water Pokémon all use water in some way. But no two Pokémon are the same. Each is strong or weak in different ways. A good trainer will pick the right one for battle. Fire may melt an ice Pokémon. But water Pokémon can put out a fire.

How do Pokémon level up?

These images show Charmander's different forms.

Charmander

Charmeleon

Charizard

Mega Charizard

Through training and battles. Pokémon often **evolve** after reaching a certain level. Special stones can also change them. Sometimes it just takes being friends with them. Evolution makes Pokémon stronger. It gives them better moves.

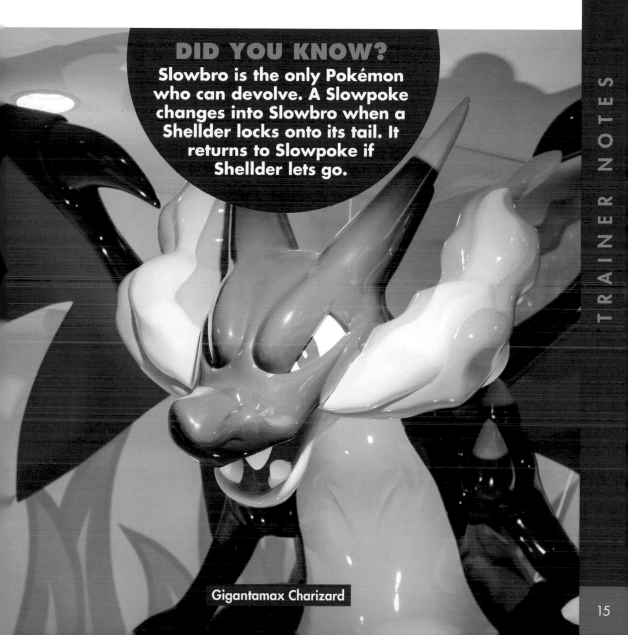

DID YOU KNOW?

Slowbro is the only Pokémon who can devolve. A Slowpoke changes into Slowbro when a Shellder locks onto its tail. It returns to Slowpoke if Shellder lets go.

Gigantamax Charizard

Can you kill a Pokémon?

Not in the card game. Pokémon never die in trainer battles. When they lose, they pass out and return to their Poké Balls. They rest and heal before they do battle again. But Pokémon can die in other ways. It happens in the **anime** and even some video games.

DID YOU KNOW?
So far, Pokémon has
20 TV series and
23 movies. It is the
longest-running
anime ever.

The movie *Pokémon
Detective Pikachu*
came out in 2019.

How many Pokémon are there?

A lot! Pokémon started with 151 characters. Since 1996, nine **generations** have been created. Each included a new land with fun new characters. Today, your **Pokédex** could total over 1,000! Gotta catch 'em all? It might take a while!

DID YOU KNOW?
The first Pokémon game hid a secret character. Find Mew, and you have 151.

Lands of the Pokémon Universe	KANTO	JOHTO	HOENN	SINNOH
	Generation 1	Generation 2	Generation 3	Generation 4
	(151 characters)	(100 characters)	(135 characters)	(107 characters)
	1996–1999	1999–2001	2002–2005	2006–2010

UNOVA	**KALOS**	**ALOLA**	**GALAR**	**PALDEA**
Generation 5	Generation 6	Generation 7	Generation 8	Generation 9
(156 characters)	(72 characters)	(88 characters)	(96 characters)	(107 characters
2010–2012	2013–2014	2016–2018	2019–2022	as of 2022)

Which is the most powerful Pokémon?

Most players agree on Arceus (ARK-ee-us). This **Legendary Pokémon** has special powers. Arceus can become any Pokémon type. It can also bring things back to life and freeze time. In play, Pokémon believe this being created their whole world. In real life, Game Freak gets that credit. Either way, Pokémon rule the gaming world!

DID YOU KNOW?

Arceus is the only Pokémon who can learn the move Judgment. This move showers meteors that totally destroy its enemy.

People young and old have fun playing Pokémon.

21

ASK MORE QUESTIONS

Which Pokémon has the most evolutions?

What are gym badges?

Try a BIG QUESTION:
What is the best strategy to become a Pokémon Master?

SEARCH FOR ANSWERS

Search the library catalog or the Internet.
A librarian, teacher, or parent can help you.

Using Keywords
Find the looking glass.

🔍

Keywords are the most important words in your question.

❓

If you want to know:

- which Pokémon has the most evolutions, type: POKÉMON MOST EVOLUTIONS
- gym badges, type: POKÉMON GYM BADGES

FIND GOOD SOURCES

Are the sources reliable?
Some sources are better than others. An adult can help you. Here are some good, safe sources.

Books
Pokémon
by Sara Green, 2018.

Pokémon: Satoshi Tajiri
by Paige V. Polinsky, 2022.

Internet Sites
Kiddle: Pokémon Facts for Kids
https://kids.kiddle.co/Pokemon
Kiddle is an online encyclopedia for kids.

Pokémon
https://www.pokemon.com/us/
Pokémon is an interactive website with games, events, online tournaments, videos, Pokédex, and brand information.

Every effort has been made to ensure that these websites are appropriate for children. However, because of the nature of the Internet, it is impossible to guarantee that these sites will remain active indefinitely or that their contents will not be altered.

SHARE AND TAKE ACTION

Hold a Pokémon contest.
Get some friends together and play with the cards or battle on a video game.

Think up a new Pokémon character.
Be sure to include where it lives, its type, some moves, and evolutions.

Talk about strategies with friends.
Picking the perfect Pokémon and moves take deep thought and practice. Together, you can come up with great ideas and become better trainers.

GLOSSARY

anime A Japanese style of cartoon.

brand A group of products made or owned by the same company.

competition A contest where two or more people are trying to win the same thing.

evolve In Pokémon, when a new character changes into one that has more power and moves.

generation A new series of Pokémon characters that lives in a certain region.

gym A stadium in a Pokémon region where trainers battle each other.

Legendary Pokémon A rare and powerful Pokémon.

Pokédex A complete list of all Pokémon characters.

quest A long search to find or do something.

rival A player you are competing against.

INDEX

About the Author

Rachel Grack has been editing and writing children's books since 1999. She lives on a small ranch in southern Arizona. She enjoys watching her grandchildren play the original Pokémon Snap and Pokémon Stadium games on her Nintendo 64 console.